John Harris Knowles

From Summer land to Summer

A Journey fFrom Thomasville, Georgia, to New York, During April and May

John Harris Knowles

From Summer land to Summer
A Journey fFrom Thomasville, Georgia, to New York, During April and May

ISBN/EAN: 9783744798389

Printed in Europe, USA, Canada, Australia, Japan

Cover: Foto ©Andreas Hilbeck / pixelio.de

More available books at **www.hansebooks.com**

A Mountain Stream in Virginia

FROM SUMMER LAND TO SUMMER

A JOURNEY FROM THOMASVILLE, GEORGIA, TO NEW YORK, DURING APRIL AND MAY, 1899, AS TOLD BY THE REV. J. HARRIS KNOWLES. WITH ILLUSTRATIONS FROM PHOTOGRAPHS BY THE REV. F. LANDON HUMPHREYS, D.D., AND MR. LUDWIG SCHUMACHER . .

NEW YORK
1899

FIVE HUNDRED COPIES PRIVATELY PRINTED
FOR FREDERICK HUMPHREYS, M.D.

No. 418

COPYRIGHT, 1899, BY
FREDERICK HUMPHREYS

TO

MRS. DR. FREDERICK HUMPHREYS,

WHOSE HAPPY IDEA LAID OUT THIS TRIP,

AND WHOSE KINDNESS

IS ALWAYS AN INSPIRATION AND A REWARD,

THESE FEW NOTES

OF A MOST ENJOYABLE TIME ARE

AFFECTIONATELY INSCRIBED

BY

J. HARRIS KNOWLES.

Contents

I

PAGE

The Rendezvous.—The Plan of the Trip.—The Pleasure of Travel.—Alone in a Pullman.—My First Fellow Traveller.—Old Acquaintances.—Chicken *à la provençale.*—New Passengers at Charleston.—The Hunters Bound for Florida.—Tales of Old Life in the South.—Returning Soldiers.—The Molested Chinaman.—Thomasville at Last 1

II

Some Days in Thomasville.—A Stroll in the Garden.—Happy, Idle Days.—Brain Pictures.—Pleasant Callers.—Southern Women.—My Little Friend.

—The Letter of Thanks.—The Country Club.—The Magnolia Road.—A Tragedy.—Sympathy for Both Sides. —Clean Content and Comfort.—The Patchwork. — The Preserves.— Susceptibility to Kindness . 29

III

Through Georgia.—The Three Zones.— The Curved Furrows.—Atlanta.—The Exposition Site.—The Gods of Greece. —Through the Town.—The Confederate Fort.—The Memorial Day Procession 59

IV

Chattanooga.—Memorable Battlefields.— Up the Incline.—On Lookout Mountain.—Through the Cemeteries.—The Graves of the Unknown.—The Great Altar 83

V

Hot Springs, Virginia.—Tennessee Moonshiners.—Mountain Ride to Springs.—

CONTENTS vii

PAGE

The Bath House.—The Mountain Valley.—The New Homestead Hotel.—Chance Meetings.—A Dead Town.—The Little Virginians . . . 103

VI

Luray Cavern.—Through the Old Town.—The Mountain Conflagration.—Our Guide. — Remembrances of War Times.—The Entrance to the Caves.—American Refinement.—Weird Light Effects.—Underground Wonders.—The Embedded Skeleton.—The Finding of the Caverns.—The Ball-room.—The Music of the Rocks.—The Cathedral.—The Chimes.—A Primeval Part.—Geological Formation.—Richness of the Pendants . 123

VII

Harper's Ferry. — Charlestown. — John Brown.—Remembrances of 1859.—Statement of Governor Wise.—Another View.—The Peace Offering.—Contrasts in the Shenandoah Valley . 145

VIII

Washington.—The Negro Singers.—The Congressional Library.—Its Gorgeousness.—The Simple Side of Things.—Near View of the Obelisk.—A Suggested Frieze. — The Payment of $20,000,000.—A Retrospect.—Conclusion 163

Illustrations

	PAGE
A Mountain Stream in Virginia . *Frontispiece*	
We hope you will be pleased with our trip . . .	iv
What do you think of it ? . .	v
A Pleasant Bit .	ix
Brynawel, Thomasville . . .	4
A Mountain Road	5
A Southern Farm	27
In the Garden, Brynawel	32
The Garden Front	33
Something worth looking at	57
Through Georgia	62
A Nickel's Worth of Niggers	63
The Circus Poster	82

ILLUSTRATIONS

	PAGE
On Lookout Mountain	86
On the Heights	87
The Incline, Chattanooga	93
The Army and the Church	102
The Waterfall	106
The Young Virginians	107
I would I were a boy again	121
Saracen's Tent *	126
Double Column *	127
Giant's Hall *	144
Harper's Ferry	148
Retrospection	149
Valley of the Shenandoah	159
Yes, we did have a lovely time	161
The Ménage	166
Heads of Departments	167
How pleasant to look back over it all!	186

* From photographs kindly furnished by Mr. Lemuel Zerkel.

The Rendezvous

OFF on our journey for the Summer Land !
   There shall we meet dear friends whose love we prize ;
   There, 'neath the glow of sunny southern skies,
True hearts will greet us, with glad outstretched hand.

True hearts, true hands, and souls who understand !
   Such are the treasures for which wisdom sighs ;
   For these, all else she evermore decries,
For, lacking these, all else is sterile sand.

Fly then, ye wheels, and fly, O speeding train,
   On from Manhattan, islanded in state ;
Fly then, ye haste me to my friends again,
   On through fair lands and cities wide and great ;
Fly then, your clamor makes a merry strain,
   On to the Home where dear friends for me wait.

J. H. K.

Brynawel, Thomasville

I

Last year it was my happiness to make "A Flight in Spring" to the Pacific Coast and back with my good friend Dr. Humphreys. The scattered notes of that ever memorable excursion have already seen the light. The preparation of them for the press was a renewal to myself of all the interest of the journey; and the assurances of pleasure derived from my little book, received from those who had read it, have more than repaid me for the labor of its production.

In this spring of 1899 my friend again called me to his side, inviting me to accompany him on his return journey from his winter home in the Southern Summer Land to his summer home in the North.

I was to join him once more at Thomasville, Georgia, and then, after a few days there, we were, with the members of his household, to take our journey northward.

Our route was to be through

Georgia; into Tennessee, stopping at Chattanooga; then into Virginia, visiting the Hot Springs; exploring the mystic beauties of the Luray Cavern; traversing the famous Shenandoah Valley; peeping at beautiful Washington; and so home, the whole affair taking about ten days.

A few of the many interesting episodes of that lovely journey I will try to reproduce.

It was, then, with a feeling of renewed pleasure that I set out on my little outing with my dear friends. Travel has always an attraction for me. When one can measure from the golden milestone of a fixed home, then to wander is ever sweet, and wandering makes the return ever sweeter.

Travel is the very easiest way to get out of the pressing sense of those immediate and never-ceasing obligations which always surround us in our ordinary affairs. But, for a journey, we can leave them all with a perfectly clear conscience. We quietly relegate them to our return.

We are, while on the wing of travel, free as the birds. We are rid of all cares. The whole world all about us is at its accustomed and inevitable toil, but we are flying through space, cared for, carried, and all the vast machinery of the universe seems to be for our unemployed leisure alone. Time even seems to be long drawn out, and without its fleeting quality. Space exists that we may pass through it; and our own will to be away and moving, thus free, seems to lift us above the world-force even of gravitation itself.

We were to meet at Thomasville. With these emotions of absolute freedom from care or obligation within me I sped on to the rendezvous.

The way was one which I traversed before, but the new spring seemed more beautiful than ever. I watched its tender buds and opening leaves, not unwillingly, from the solitude of a Pullman.

I was the only passenger on board until we reached Philadelphia. Travel in the through cars south was light. To be thus alone after the roar of New York was delightful. I gave myself up to it much as the gentleman did who thought that the height of pleasure was to be alone in the choir of an English cathedral, while organ and choristers and chanting priests filled the vast sacred space with holy sound. The rhythmic throb of the engine and the continuous murmur of the wheels were not out of keeping with my peaceful rest, while through the windows I could see how spring was once more decking itself in living green.

It did not take me long to scrape an acquaintance with the solitary fellow traveller who came on board at the Broad Street Station in Philadelphia. We were soon in pleasant conversation, and by one of those curious combinations in life, I found that he was the son of a Chicago physician whom I had known well, many years before.

There was no dearth of topic or of talk on the rest of our journey together, which was as far as Baltimore. We had much to say of friends who were no more; of lives with downward trend, and of those whose years were brighter ever as they neared the close.

Then there was business to be talked of; and the questions of the day; and higher things were not forgotten. I remember how my friend's eyes were humid as he spoke of his dear wife and her religious zeal, and of her scrupulous care of his children; but, said he, fingering a rather large and somewhat artistic emblem of a well-known secret society, "This gives me all the religion I want." But as he said the words I could feel that there was in them rather a bravado tone and not the genuine ring of a firm conviction.

"No," said I, "that does not, nor can it ever satisfy you. You have taken that up of your own free will. It has just as much authority as you wish to give it. It is in your control. Religion is something different. It must seize your whole being. You must regard it as having power over you, whether you wish it or not, and that it is from God, whose you are, and whom you must serve."

He listened to me with profound regard, and, as he looked afar out of the car window, he spoke of the difficulties of faith and of certain things which seemed to him unreasonable, but he admitted that the devotion of his wife, and his love for his children, made him wish to believe. We soon parted. Baltimore was close at hand, where he left me with a warm shake of the hand, and once more I was in the magnificence of the Pullman all alone.

The time soon came for that which it is never safe to neglect on a journey, one's dinner. Perhaps this pressing need is left with mortals *en route*, to remind them that, despite of all their freedom from ordinary cares and entanglements, for the nonce, they yet are human.

The lonesome darkies were glad to have something to do, when I called them to my side and told my wants. I found that I was in a buffet car. The waiter presented me with enthusiasm the ornamental menu. Thereon was an alluring array of dishes, with rather mixed lingual names. Chicken à *la provençale* tempted me, but it was a rash venture. It was a horrid mess of fibrous substance, out of which the bones dropped too easily; and the reddish tomatoes and scattering spices did not add anything attractive to the dish.

"Your chicken à *la provençale* does not amount to much," I said to the attendant.

"No, sah," was the reply; "dem canned goods ain't no good."

Here was a near reflection of "Embalmed Beef" right with me; and what visions did it bring up!

"Is everything on this menu canned?" I asked.

"Yes, sah, ebrything 'cept ham and tongue," was the reply.

Then said I, "Serve me ham or tongue for the rest of the journey."

What an absurd glitter of a Parisian café the promising menu gave, but all dropped in prosaic fact, into a cupboard of canned goods and a kerosene oil stove therein, to warm them up for the use of innocent and incautious passengers.

All this, however, was a mere trifling grievance to any man with either head or heart, for by this time we were speeding on through the historic soil of Virginia. From the windows of my lonely car there were ever pictures to be seen. The great curves of the ploughed fields; the old houses nestling in their surrounding trees; the mixture of new and old in the stations we passed through; the historic names and places which came to our eyes as we flew along; all gave something to think of, to dream of, or to hope for. How, everywhere in such a great State, the past, the present, and the future come to gaze at you, a mystic three, indissolubly linked together!

It was not until next morning at Charleston, that any great increase was made to our company. During the night a few passengers had entered; but, once in the real South, every seat was occupied. The greater number were on pleasure bent; off for outings at Brunswick, or fishing in Florida. With a group of the fishermen I soon found myself in agreeable chat; not that I am a fisherman, for I prefer the pleasure of the woods and streams, pure and simple, to any hunt for game or anything else that you can trap or kill therein. The thirst to do to death anything one sees in the woods seems to me inexplicable. I would rather be able to get close to bird and beast, and see how they live, and learn something of their mysterious existence, than thus to slay them.

Even the wanton destruction of plant or flower seems a sort of sacrilege ; there is a veneration for nature in that self-restraint which can

"Love the wild rose, and leave it on its stem."

A certain nobleness does, however, inhere in the hunter, and out of his excess and riot in killing, some good does come. Among my hunting fellow travellers I picked out one for his splendid bearing. Tall, graceful, every movement harmonious, with steady eye, and good health gleaming from his clear complexion. When I entered the smoking-room of the car, he at once courteously asked if tobacco was disagreeable to me. Of course it was not. A lighted cigar soon made me free of the company.

It was then I learned of the proposed fishing excursion to Florida, in which a young Englishman with him was to take part. I hoped they would get the biggest tarpon known, but it seems they were after smaller game.

As we journeyed on my new-found and most courteous friend told me of the old life among the Sea Islands, off from Charleston and that region. From plantation to plantation the lords of the soil went in eight-oared gigs to make brave pleasure for themselves under hospitable roofs.

One can easily imagine how the cup might overflow now and then, and that hot blood would assert itself in rather positive ways; but, like a dream, it has all vanished, and a new order rises and new problems come, more difficult to settle than when black and white marked the lines.

In relation to all this my friend told me that in those old days a book appeared, written by the young English wife of a Southern planter, which antedated "Uncle Tom's Cabin" and had almost as widespread an influence in England as Mrs. Harriet Beecher Stowe's famous story years afterward. The work of the young Englishwoman was, however, largely a collection of "dreadful tales" which she had heard from the rollicking and mischievously exaggerating lips of the boon companions of her husband. Her horrors were a spur to their invention, and tales which might have adorned the "Arabian Nights" were so positively affirmed that she believed them.

One was related to me by my hunter friend. It was in brief this: Two planters have an affair of honor. A duel is to decide all. The details of weapons, and all that I forget, but the crowning condition was that all the slaves of the vanquished were to be killed by the victor, beheaded, and their heads used by him, to ornament the fence-posts of his plantation. This wild story is a specimen of what was credited and printed.

The hours of travel all through the day were made bright by the genial conversation of my hunter friend. At Waycross—where I was to leave the main line for the local branch to Thomasville—just before changing cars, my new-found friend sought me out and bade me farewell with all the warmth of an old acquaintance.

Strange as it may seem, we found during our previous conversation that we both alike knew the same people in England, and had been guests under the same roof in that hospitable and lovely land.

It so happened that in our vivid chat and pleasant interchange of thought we quite overlooked exchanging cards. His name I know not, neither does he know mine, but I shall always remember him with most pleasant recollections.

The journey from Waycross to Thomasville was passed in the ordinary day coaches. In them one came more directly in contact with the ordinary life of the people. It was somewhat of a tedious journey, though there was quite enough to interest and amuse, nevertheless.

On board was quite a sprinkling of returning soldiers, some listless and indifferent looking. Doubtless, the horrors of drill camps, and the experience of hastily equipped troops under a tropic sun, had had their effect upon them. There was one tall, gaunt boy among them with a fearful cough, who seemed able to make sport enough for all. Fever and consumption were marked upon his hollow cheeks, but nothing could dampen his good humor and energy. He was here, there, everywhere; hail fellow, well met, with everyone. Once, when a Chinaman entered the car and slipped quietly into his seat, the young soldier greeted him with derisive cries of "Washee, washee." I could not help leaning over and saying in a low voice to my young friend who was thus mocking the stranger: "How would you like to be made game of if you were out in China?" The young man's own good heart made answer for him by his silence at my remark, and his further silence also toward the Chinaman for the rest of the journey.

The hours sped on, taking us westward through the rich level lands of southern Georgia, until, in due time, we were once more at our rendezvous in Thomasville.

Some Days in Thomasville

A PILLARED porch, a garden all around,
   Tall whisp'ring trees, and glowing skies above,
   Long rose-lined alleys, breathing peace and love,
Bright flowers and mocking-birds for sight and sound.

A noble hall, whose space gives welcome sweet,
   To those who enter its wide-open door;
   A hint it seems of that fair tranquil shore,
Where loved ones welcome, and where angels greet.

And then, " the many mansions " of the blest,
   What are they, but the chambers where we sleep!
   In peaceful mystery of slumber deep,
Each wrapped about, and tenderly caressed.
A pillared porch, a garden all around,
Where flowers and gracious deeds alike abound.

J. H. K.

In the Garden, Brynawel

II

Once more in Thomasville, it was delightful to drive through the embowered streets, to the hospitable home which awaited me. There it stood, under its huge trees, in its fragrant garden; and under the broad shadow of its pillared portico were my welcoming friends.

After the first few words of greeting were said it seemed that one's first duty in coming from the North was at once to visit the roses and the flowers. There was a touch of melancholy in this garden ramble, for during the past winter an icy blast had blown from the dark depths of air, and had killed many of the choicest and exotic flowery shrubs. It was the biggest "freeze," everybody said, which had been known for years. The great creeper on the portico was no more. The perfumed veil of its foliage had disappeared; but nature is never discouraged. Already great shoots were striking up and out, and six inches, or more, in one night was no uncommon growth. How curious it would be if our ears were so acute as to be able to hear the impact of the increase in growing organisms, as the cells expand and atom joins on to atom. I have fancied, in a close night in August, that one could really hear the corn grow during the dark stillness of the silent hours. It was all a series of fitful creaks and starts, and mysterious rustlings among the tall stalks of the growing corn, while not a breath of air was moving; and yet there was ever perceptible this strange "going," as in the tops of the mulberry trees, in the scripture story.

Happy were the idle days passed under the sapphire sky of southern Georgia. There was nothing to do but lounge and drive, and rest in peace. I painted pictures for myself by the score, and all this without material canvas or color, or one movement of the body from the veranda chair.

No artist could seize such pictures in their fleeting splendor, except with the sudden process of a photographic look. Thus, with my eyes for object glasses, and the dark chamber of the brain for camera obscura, I tried to capture all the beauties of earth and air which surrounded me.

Up through the great masses of the evergreen oaks one could look at the sky, whose hue was of the deepest blue imaginable, with a rich tone in it of surpassing softness; while floating across its illimitable depths were mountainous clouds, all creamy white and golden, suggestive of rest and repose, and tender, loving warmth. The whole picture as seen from that veranda chair was a delight for ever—the rich tone of the reddish earth in the open roadway, the intermingled greens of the herbage and shrubs, culminating in the dark masses of the oaks, outlined against the sapphire sky, and the moving masses of the regal clouds. From morn till night, from east, back again to east, this panorama of beauty was unfolding itself. To enjoy it all no more was needed than the shifting of one's chair and the opening of one's eyes to the overwhelming splendor of it all.

Another picture which I must preserve was a view over the Ockloconee River. We came one day upon the stream, in one of our drives, and from the vantage ground of a tall bridge we could take in the bizarre effect of the scene. The banks were wooded and precipitous. The tortuous river bed lay among sand banks almost white, against which the clear water, brown and transparent as the complexion of a handsome mulatto, lay in tranquil depths. These depths were veritable mirrors for trees and clouds and skies, but the reflections in the water were all strangely changed. They appeared in a clear monochrome, as if painted in bitumen. The whole effect was beautiful. Above was the clear blue sky, the vivid and varied green of the foliage, the broken ground of the banks in reddish tints, the sand banks glittering white in the sunlight; while in the still depths of the water all was reflected in minute detail, but changed to this mysterious unity of uniform brown. Somebody has said of old-time landscape painters that their idea of green grass was the color of an old violin. Here was just such a landscape, all painted by nature itself, in the depths of the Ockloconee.

But one could not give all one's time to those pleasant reveries. The portico was the scene of many a pleasant call from Southern friends, sorry to take their leave of pleasant neighbors, who in a day or two would leave this Southern summer land for the summer of their far-off Northern home. Such calls were delightful. What can be more enjoyable than the free, easy flow of refined conversation, gliding on from topic to topic, as a clear stream winds through a landscape, reflecting the form and color of all that moves or grows upon its banks? Certainly the Southern women have wonderful talents in this relation, and their soft voices and bright eyes give value and emphasis to their every utterance.

I had a little experience with a very little lady during one of my strolls in the garden. We were separated by the fence, the little lady and myself. She was playing with a big black dog, who, on the appearance of another dog following some colored men, heedlessly ran away from his little mistress. Disconsolately she called after him, "Nero, Nero," but he did not return. Then in louder tones she called "Nigger, Nigger," at which her truant dog returned. My little friend explained to me that her dog was first called "Nigger," but her mamma had changed it to "Nero," and that he did not know his name very well yet. I was amused at the adroitness which, by turning the dog's name into Italian, had preserved his identity and avoided a term which might give offence. We had a great chat together. That was last spring. I told her where I had come from, and where we were bound for, at which her eager eyes opened wide. "Well," said she, "there is one place in Philadelphia I would like to see, and that is Wanamaker's. They have everything there." Then there was talk of all the toys there, and it ended by my promising her that when I got back to New York I would send her a little toy that I knew would please her, and that was a dear little doll baby in a bath tub, that she could wash and dress every time she wished. But alas, I lost the memorandum of her name, and the whole thing dropped from my memory until one day during this visit, looking up from the portico, I saw my dear little girl once more. After drawing her into conversation, and cautiously leading up to toys, she told me that last year "an old man" had told her that he would send her a dolly in a bath tub from New York, and said she, with a melancholy far-off air, "He never did." I asked her if she thought I looked like that old man, and in an amazed and amused manner she said "You do!"

Well, it is needless to say that after I got back to New York one of my first visits was to a toy shop, where I made my purchase and duly dispatched it by mail to my little friend.

In due time this charming letter reached me in reply, full of kind feeling and that flow of language ever a power on the lips of a Southern woman :

THOMASVILLE GA
5—19—1899—

REV J HARRIS KNOWLES

Kind Friend you made a little South Georgia girl very happy the other day by sending her the sweet little doll and bath tub yes they came safe and sound and I thank you very much for them and shall keep them a long time I hope you had a Pleassant trip home and are all well it is very dry and hot and disty here now We have not had rain for a long time and the gardens are all dried up I hope to see you down here next winter I am going to read the book you wrote that Mama liked so well A Flight In Spring I spent four days last winter in New Orleans and liked it very much PaPa is taking out fresh honey every day wish you had some With kind wishes and many thanks I remain your little Friend

A. R.

Among the memorable drives during my few days at Thomasville was one out to the Country Club and another on the Magnolia Road.

The Country Club stands on a high knoll from which one sees out over a rich wooded landscape of splendid vistas. The grounds are extensive, up hill and down dale in constant change. The golf grounds are gay during the winter season, and the mild climate gives constant opportunity for out-door sports. The dark pools and knotted vines overhanging them, in the forest dells, were picturesque and mysterious, but in summer heats might not be inviting.

The ride on Magnolia Road was one to be remembered. It was under the umbrageous trees. The roadway almost lost itself in the thickets; the magnolia flowers were yet in bud, but the day was warm, and the lizards on the fence-posts, as they stuck out for the moment, like bits of dried bark, rigid and immovable, but ever ready to devour the passing flies, gave hint of that struggle for life which ever surrounds us, and which finds its most dreadful emphasis in those lands which near themselves to the tropics.

It seems to me that all life, especially in its tragic aspects, increases in intensity as one nears the equator. Here in Georgia, under the bright skies and the languor of the clear atmosphere, there was the heavy feeling of a tragedy just past, the culminating horror of many such. The public prints from the great centres were full of fearful details, but the local paper, with rare good sense, omitted all these, yet, nevertheless, the lurid horror stared us in the face for all that.

The consciousness of that tragedy at Newnan, Georgia, which took place under the light of the Sunday just past, filled one with sorrow—sorrow first and foremost for the good people of Georgia —the gentle, the just, the wise, as, held in the grip of an inevitable destiny, they have to face the fearful complications of their surroundings. My thoughts reverted to the crowds of colored people, in increasing numbers, which I saw as I came farther South. They lounged about the depots; they lolled from the windows in the streets of the little towns; they seemed to wear a heedless, defiant air or to bear themselves with a coarse indifference so apparently foreign to the usual confiding and yielding nature of the negro. It was dreadful.

Over against all this one could put the indomitable will of the yet master race, which ever must master or die, and the dreadful complications possible in Southern life under all these conditions. I confess that my heart was in my mouth, in the sympathy which was within me; sympathy for those who had inherited these complications, and who had to face the fearful problems which confronted them; sympathy for the white people of the South, with all the burthen which they have to bear.

But there was sympathy too for the colored man. I could not but note the difficulties of his sad fate, and how hopeless seems his outlook, notwithstanding what he may accomplish for his own advancement. He has done much. He has achieved wonders in his own development. The world has not seen a parallel condition to that which has passed under our eyes during the last thirty years. No enslaved race, suddenly freed, could have accomplished so much as the colored people have in their educational progress in these United States. But the tragedy of it all is that this progress does not smooth away difficulties in social conditions, but rather emphasizes them.

It may be that political issues work much harm in the mutual relations between whites and blacks in the South. Time must be then the great healer. Meanwhile one must admit that it is a fearful thing to be ever brought face to face with a constantly increasing factor in the social state, compared with which the dangerous and ignorant portions of our Northern communities, even in our most crowded cities, are as nothing. It is a terrible thing to exploit the colored masses of the South for any party ends whatever. It should be frowned down by all true lovers of our country.

Turning from these troubled thoughts I have a lovely memory of some happy colored people I met. What could be better than their clean content, their white floors, their spotless bedspreads, their daintily dressed windows, and the glittering array of their kitchens! They had their gardens too, where roses grew as well as vegetables, the onion and the sweet pea side by side, the useful and the beautiful. Proudly the mistress of the establishment showed us the completed ambition of her needle—a silk patchwork which took the prize at the county fair. There was a touch of pathos in her words when she told us that she got the blue ribbon all right for that, and her preserves, but the money prize was omitted, for "there war'nt any." As to the preserves, these were veritable works of art, I suppose never to be eaten, but to be looked at with awe. What triumph there was as the great crystal jars were placed in our hands for our inspection! There were preserved watermelon rind and cantelopes, all carved over in intaglio, showing fishes and leaves and graceful ornaments. It was really artistic. When I asked Mrs. B. how she did it, she answered with a laugh, "Oh, I jes' did it," and that was all one could elicit. I was much interested in this display of taste in its double sense, taste for the sweets and taste for the clever ornamentation thereon.

I afterwards learned that among the colored people there is always a great reluctance to tell the process by which they accomplish anything. There is a sort of superstition that if they tell they lose the knack themselves for ever. This idea has place, if I mistake not, in a far wider circle than the negro race, and may be at the bottom of trade secrets.

Among my many pleasant impressions of Thomasville the happy home of these faithful colored people, trusting and trusted servants, is not the least.

There is no race that is so amenable to kindness as our negro population. What but this susceptibility can explain the loyalty of the Southern slaves during the trying years from 1862 to 1865? Everything on the plantations was then in their hands, but then the colored people, in their position of trust, were the protectors, the providers, the loving support of those they looked up to and respected. There was no violence, no outrage, no fearful crime. There was a bond of mutual dependence and respect.

Despite of all present difficulties, if I mistake not, the Southern people have even now more kindly feeling instinctively to the negroes than the people of the North, for they know them better, are accustomed to them, and understand them.

Through Georgia

Despite of all the glory of the State,
    The swelling billows of the fertile land,
    Wealth like of India, or of Samarcand,
Yet did my heart at times feel desolate.

Who shall unwind the knots of dreadful fate,
    Who shall mete justice out with even hand,
    Who shall with power, all evil men withstand,
Who shall defend the honor of the State!

O land of Whitfield, Wesley, Oglethorpe,
    O land where mercy was a corner-stone,
    Think not that blood, rash spilt, can e'er atone.
The pang of mercy may be keen and sharp,
    And stricken hearts may weep and sadly moan,
    But love, and justice, can prevail alone.

                            J. H. K.

Through Georgia

III

OUR passage through Georgia, that Empire State of the South, was something to be remembered.

As we travelled northward and westward from Thomasville in the south, to Chattanooga just over the line of the State, in Tennessee, we traversed the three great zones of Georgia—the great sandy plain which rises gradually from the Atlantic sea coast, extending as far as Macon; then, a hilly and diversified region, looking like a pleasant and healthy district; and lastly, the mountainous country, which has its culmination on Lookout Mountain in Tennessee.

The impression made upon one by this great journey of more than three hundred miles was that one was looking at an empire in very truth. In the north were mountain fastnesses, picturesque and even sublime. Here were the sources of the two principal rivers which traverse the land. Here were rich mineral deposits, gold even having been found in paying quantities in the past. Here, too, were the scenes of some of the highest developments of life among the American Indians, but, above all other causes of interest, this vast and romantic region was the scene of the bloodiest and most deadly contests between the North and South during the Civil War.

Through all this great Empire State, with its history and vast resources, we made our flying trip, resting only once at Atlanta, and once again, just at the northern entrance of the State, in Chattanooga, Tennessee.

We saw with our eyes what the books tell us—that Georgia can produce everything that all the

States of the Union can produce, with the exception of a few semi-tropical products peculiar to the neighboring State of Florida.

We travelled northward through the great sandy, pine-clad plain, rich in its timber and also capable of profitable cultivation, until darkness settled down upon us. When morning dawned we were in a hilly region of rich red loam, somewhat exhausted, we were told, by successive crops, but yet capable of profitable cultivation.

This part of the State has a certain grandiose air about it. The billowy lines of the ever-ascending hills, with the constant evidences of agriculture all about one, gave an idea of largeness and proportionate prosperity which we hoped was realized in fact. The whole country had a character of its own—broad, breezy, and luminous. Somehow, one forgot to look out for houses or towns or stations as our way wound through this great full-breasted country, so rich and opulent-looking in its possibilities.

I noticed one peculiarity in the agriculture which set me thinking. It was this: Through all the stretches of ploughed land through which we passed I could not find a field with a straight, even furrow. The traces left by the ploughshare were all in curved lines. Every hillside, every bending area, had its curved lines upon it. They followed the slightest deviation of the surface from a dead level. Even where the field was flat, there too the lines would curve in a way that would bring horror to the heart of a Northern farmer. I watched these graceful tattooings on the earth's surface with a curious interest. On some of the hillsides the plough marks were as involved almost as the peculiar lines which each man carries on the end of his thumb.

I asked some people I met what was the cause of this peculiarity, and was told that this variation from the straight line was probably to prevent washouts on the hillsides. But that did not seem reasonable to me, for the graceful curvatures were everywhere. The field might be as flat as a table, but the ploughshare wabbled round there just the same; and a straight line in a furrow in Georgia was as hard to find as a straight line anywhere in nature's great handiwork, whether in plant, animal, or man.

I fell back finally upon a theory of my own as to the cause of all these graceful curves in the ploughed fields of Georgia. They are, said I, the results of the instinctively artistic temperament of the negro workman. He loves rhythmic motion. It exists in his speech, in his songs, in his gait— there is something repugnant to him in the monotony of a straight line. He never will follow it. He prefers the variation from the inflexible. He hates rules and all routine, and relieves himself in the tediousness of agricultural labor by those artistic curves which the ploughshare in his hands is made to produce. The sign-manual of a nature pleasure-loving, indeterminate, ever lightening labor with an instinctive sense of beauty, lies all over the State of Georgia.

How different it was in Tennessee; how much more marked the straight line was in Virginia! How clean and clear it cleaves through the soil of New England, or stretches its vast parallels on our Western prairies! How exact it is on the ploughed lands of our Old Home, finding its most exact conditions when the ploughshare is guided by the firm hand and cool head of a Scotch farmer on the fields of Ayrshire or the slopes of Midlothian!

I believe that the curved furrows of Georgia tell us deep truths of racial peculiarities, worthy of our earnest study. To plough, and keep ploughing, a straight furrow requires steady persistence, an intelligent, resolute will, and a power of concentration—all which qualities pertain especially to superior races of men.*

We were prepared to find in Atlanta, Georgia, where we stayed over a day, a thoroughly wide-awake place. It is a typical centre of the new South. When one sees the handsome avenues of well-built mansions, and the busy streets in the business portions of the city, it is hard to realize that the ravages of war had passed over the place, not so long since, with both fire and sword, and almost razed it to the ground.

* My theory of line variation is worth a thought, but since writing the above, I have been again assured by a Georgian that the curved furrows were to prevent washouts, and to conserve moisture.

The enterprise and spirit of the little place rather surprises some other towns in Georgia. It is considered a clear case of bluff, and the audacity which conceived the "World's Fair" Exposition, recently held there, and for which "an appropriation" was asked and obtained, completely took the breath away from less progressive centres.

We went out to the exposition grounds, and saw them in their melancholy decay. Exposed laths and broken plaster dispelled the magnificent illusion of "marble palaces and cloud-capped towers." But one could imagine the stage all set and the crowd playing

"World's Fair" to their own satisfaction, and the lining of some pockets at least.

Even in its decay one could see what a really good thing it must have been, and though as nothing to the Columbian Exposition, yet it was a surprising success within its own limits.

It was curious to see a faded tympanum on the façade of one of the buildings, with the gods of Greece and the myths of the ancients still dominating the intellect and art of this our modern day. It is the infinitesimal which has undying potency. Little Greece and little Athens, with her great men and greater artists, a mere handful amid the myriads of the world, still rule over us in æsthetic relations and vitalize all that we have of artistic conception or power.

Our day at Atlanta coincided with Memorial Day, when the South yearly renews her devotion to her sleeping soldiers. In the morning of that day we extended our excursion beyond the site of the exposition through the residence portion of the town out to Grant Park and to the site of the old Confederate fort, on a commanding eminence, where the cannon remain as they did in those days of strife, which we trust can never again be renewed.

It is a thrilling thing to stand on a site, made dreadful and sacred both, by the blood of men; to bring before one's mind, under that calm, peaceful sky above one, that on that very spot were turmoil and encounter, the clash of arms, and the tread of death.

We returned to the centre of the little city and passed some hours just lounging about the streets. The Memorial Day procession was to come off later on in the afternoon, and hot as the day was we determined to see it. The papers gave the names of the various notables who took part, the order of their precedence, and the various organizations marching in the lines. But I preferred to look on as an utter stranger and take in the impression of the moment.

It was worth noticing how intense and real the interest was in the whole proceeding. Flags were everywhere, the Union flag, of course, on all buildings, but in the hands of the people on the streets and in the line were small Confederate flags of various styles. I tried in vain to find one to purchase in the stores; there were none on sale.

At last the procession hove in sight, and at the head was a marked and stern figure. He was cheered to the echo, and bowed right and left with chevalier-like grace. His empty sleeve, pinned to his breast, told the story. The ease with which he managed his spirited horse with one hand revealed his power. His gaunt, thin face, prominent nose, determined eyebrows, and well-marked cheek bones, all told their tale of daring, endurance, and persistence. But his staff was more interesting even than himself. It consisted of striplings, each a six-footer, each easy and erect in his saddle, each a soldier, and yet little more than a boy. On they followed their old scarred leader. He was bowing right and left, but they were impassive, eyes to the front, immovable, sword at rest, young eaglets, with all the blood, brain, and bravery of the old bird before them.

There were various military companies, cavalry and infantry, among the latter a colored regiment, loudly applauded. The line was swelled with various civic organizations, all bearing flowers and wreaths to deck the graves of the departed. This duty was not left alone to the military. A distinguishing and pleasing part of the procession was a lengthy and double line of carriages, filled with ladies, who were to take their part in the memorial services of the day. It gave one's heart a tug to see the mourning garb of some, their silvered hair and their bent forms; but love was undying within them. The young, too, were with them to ensure the continuance of the same love when they were gone. O, how women's hearts are ever true to departed memories! It was delightful, here in Atlanta, to see that the place was not too big to thrust out from its Memorial Day procession the loving hands of the truly gentle, as well as the truly bereaved.

The great procession passed on, with music and flowers, and the combined flags of the Union and the Confederacy; the first, a glorious fact, more loved than ever, the other, a memory, but cherished and revered for its very daring, the symbol of a cause whose success would have been ruin, but whose overthrow was nevertheless bitter at the time.

Out of that bitterness has come the new wine of a recognized and national life, and in that life may Atlanta, and all the South, ever flourish.

At night we drew out of the city and by morning we were " through Georgia," and at Chattanooga in Tennessee.

Chattanooga

An altar high within the land,
Where erstwhile foes stand hand in hand,
Tears now unite—They understand.

The love of country each inspired,
With honor high each soul was fired,
The fame of each, by each, is quired.

An altar tomb within the land,
To martyred dead, a glorious band,
Whom all can claim, hand grasped in hand.

J. H. K.

On Lookout Mountain

IV

CHATTANOOGA, just over the northern border of Georgia, in Tennessee, is a place filled with interest.

It lies at the foot of Lookout Mountain, and is in the centre of scenes ever memorable in the history of the United States.

From this point one can go to the battle-fields of Chickamauga, Missionary Ridge, Orchard Knob, and Lookout Mountain; and when one speaks of these sites, he speaks not merely of localities, but of places which would be interesting even if the raven wing of war had never overshadowed them. Nature here is lavish in the immense, in the picturesque, in the inspiring; but when one adds to this the fact that only thirty-six years ago, in the short space of three months and nine days, 34,000 men laid down their lives here, within the radius of one's glance, as one stands on Lookout Mountain, then, indeed, the whole place seems filled with ghosts. One is thrilled by the vast expanse of the view; but the deeper thrill is that of one's soul, as the eye within sees not the landscape merely, but the strife, the tumult, the shouts of battle, and the garments steeped in blood.

It all seemed incredible as one looked out over that great expanse of the fair surface of the earth. How could blood have been spilt under such a sky? How could men, on those inspiring mountain heights, hurl each other down the declivities to certain death? Yet so it was. The very clouds which hung upon the mountains, covering both armies, seemed loath to lift themselves from the serried lines, obscured from each other by the merciful mists of heaven.

But time moved on inexorably, and the clear light came, and brothers slew each other, until night again came down to hide from each their awful work.

Yes, it was glory, it was bravery, it was the noble offering of a nation's best blood; but though it was all this, it need not have been. So at least one may venture to think; but the gage of war was thrown down, and the delirium of that fearful madness must needs have its end.

It was then, with hearts attuned to the unseen influences of all that historic reality, that we went out to see it all, as it is to-day.

The town of Chattanooga, a

railroad centre of no mean importance, the site of several large industrial establishments, presented an animated appearance. Its well-paved streets, attractive residences, and general air of prosperity gave one pleasure. It was a mere outpost before the war, but ever since the dawn of peace it has gone on increasing in importance as the years fly by. It bids fair to be always an attractive centre, commercially and socially. Commercially it is the gateway to the great railroad systems of the South; socially it is already attractive as affording both a summer and winter residence amid scenes of romantic beauty and historic interest.

Our first point was up to the top of Lookout Mountain. We made this ascent by one of the inclined railways, of almost perpendicular grade, having near its termination an ascent of sixty-seven feet in one hundred. One has an instinctive tendency to cling pretty closely to the seats in this section of the incline; for, as one looks out over the vast landscape beneath one, it would seem as if an uneasy jerk would spill the passengers into space.

We made the upward journey with perfect safety and great rapidity. One would have preferred the leisurely ascent, by the continuous windings of the well-kept

The Incline, Chattanooga

military road, but that would take up too much time. Once on the great mountain plateau we were unmindful of aught else but the historic memories we had brought with us, and the noble expanse which spread itself out at our feet.

An old negro was our cicerone for the occasion. He had been all through the war, he said, and told us with his soft voice his story of the battles, which I have completely forgotten. The one thing which sticks to me is that, while speaking of other military heroes as gen'ral this, or gen'ral that, he always spoke of Grant as *Giant* Grant.

It was hopeless to get from him

any clear idea of the lines of attack and defence, except in a most scattered way. It was better to give one's self up to the scene, and let imagination work.

As far as possible the positions of the various regiments engaged in the several battles have been determined, and marked by suitable monumental stones and bronze tablets. The whole vast extent of the battle sites has been thus marked by loving and patriotic hands. But these waymarks of history require for their present use a previous knowledge of the whole campaign and the actors therein, which everyone does not possess.

It was delightful, however, to think that at the close of the war both sides united at once in the respectful and reverential duty of thus identifying these historic localities. The eleven Federal and eleven Confederate States whose troops were engaged here in mortal combat have united to conserve their dust, to perpetuate their names, and to preserve the memories of their patriotism and bravery.

Not only have battle monuments been raised by these States to the brave departed, but the bodies of the slain have been lovingly gathered and laid to sleep beneath the green sward of vast cemeteries, whose grace and beauty speaks ever of peace.

Through cemetery after cemetery we drove, each one more beautiful than the other, and this beauty came not from any meretricious ornamentation or park gardening. It was rather the result of nature's own sympathy. It came from the rich green sward, from the over-arching trees, and from that air of sombre magnificence which the great spaces presented.

In no other nation, if I mistake not, could one find such evidences of grateful love, to officers and soldiers alike, as one finds in our national military cemeteries, wherever they are found. This is more touchingly manifested where the very battle-field itself or its immediate vicinity has been selected for such loving remembrance. Here at Chattanooga the rank and file, as well as generals and officers, were all individually commemorated. Whether under the massive monument, or in the narrow grave, the individual man was remembered. His name and style were there engraven. But love did not stay even at this. There were many soldiers left unidentified. The tramp of battle and the rapid sweep of the succeeding hours often removed all traces of likeness, and made recognition impossible. To gather all those up and put them in one common grave would have seemed enough to some, but that did not suffice the love that followed their fate and mourned for them. Hence it is, that the most touching sights in Chattanooga Cemetery are the sweeping curves of the nameless graves which mark the last resting places of the unknown dead.

Unknown they were, but their personal identity, even though unknown, was respected and honored. There was nothing that touched me more in the national cemetery than those graves. The manner in which they were placed, the sense of beauty in the great curving lines in which they lay, all told a story of loving and tender sentiment not met with, I think, under other skies.

It would have been pleasant to linger for days at Chattanooga, to inspect its industries of iron and lumber, its manufactories of farming implements and other industries, to visit its many churches, and schools, and know more of its growing life, but we had to hurry on, despite even of some pressing invitations to tarry longer.

It would have been a delight to have taken a leisurely outlook over all those historic sites, and intelligently to trace out how battles were lost and won. We had, however, seen enough to inspire our souls with thoughts of glory and of country, and to fill our imagination with the idea that Lookout Mountain was as a great altar set up in the midst of our land, ever sacred to union and to peace, upon which a precious offering had been placed by the whole nation, which would make another such war between brethren, forever impossible.

Hot Springs, Virginia

From the dark depths of earth
　　Come genial, living springs;
Like angels from the vast profound
　　With healing on their wings.

From the mysterious deep
　　Which eye hath never seen;
The healing waters issue forth,
　　Translucent, clear, serene.

They come to heal, to bless,
　　To give us joy for pain;
To tell us that in every deep,
　　Is blessing, for our gain.

Out of the deep of woe,
　　Can come the balm of peace;
Out of the deep of death,
　　For every ill, surcease.

　　　　　　　　　　J. H. K.

The Waterfall

V

We went by night through the picturesque regions of east Tennessee, and doubtless missed much thereby. I had heard from my hunting friend, whom I met on his way to Florida, many interesting things about this wild country and its primitive inhabitants.

To their unsophisticated nature the legislation which restricts the free transmutation of corn into whiskey seems a most unreasonable proceeding. For the original bushel of the simple corn they can procure but a trifling and fluctuating price; but for the distilled juice thereof they can always command a ready and eager market, and obtain an ever so much larger income.

The light of day, when excise officers are on the alert, is not as welcome to them as the hours when moonlight casts its shadows. Hence, I presume, their name of "Moonshiners," which in this poetic fashion refers to their concealed and illicit traffic.

A man travelling in these regions must be ready at a moment's notice to answer very clearly as to what his business is, where he comes from, and whither he is going. Woe betide him if there is any mystery in his movements, or if he cannot clear his skirts of any suspicion of being an exciseman.

The traffic in these spirits of the night is carried on with a fine sense of honor. A man leaves his jug, with the necessary money, at a certain place, and in the silence and mystery of darkness his vessel, filled, is left in his outhouse, or barn, or some convenient spot where it is sure to be found. It is all very rude and simple, and I suppose in a certain sense immoral, but it is very interesting.

My hunting friend told me of an old aunt of his who lived in those parts. She was a grand dame of the old school, and lived in fine state. At her death it was my friend's duty to settle her estate. As they overhauled her premises they found demijohn after demijohn tucked away in all sorts of places. They were all full, untouched; and when the caretaker of the place was asked for an explanation of such singular storage, his answer was, that the old lady was so anxious to keep the whiskey away from him, that every demijohn she could lay hands on she hid thus away.

It is no wonder that such regions and such people give material for some of our best native romances written. We were sorry we could not see them all at closer view.

In due time we left the main line of the railroad, and made the ascent on the very steep and very select railway leading to the celebrated Hot Springs in Virginia.

The ride was interesting, even after all the experiences of the Far West and Colorado. There was no such wildness or grandeur as one sees there, but yet it was all inspiring and beautiful.

We nestled down for the night, in that narrow mountain fastness, enjoying the comfort of our private car, but not before we had made a little tour of observation, taking in, as far as possible, all the advantages of the place. The hot springs in use are all enclosed in a spacious bath-house, immediately connecting with the New Homestead Hotel. Next day we made experience of the baths, and certainly nothing could be better than the warm and beautifully crystalline, greenish water, clear and pure as the air. The bathing facilities are splendid and tasteful, without any luxurious display, or suggestion even of voluptuousness. The lavish clear flow of the warm waters was delightful, and it seemed that it must be a fountain of health to all who could try to make their inner lives as clean as its cleansing flood. There were lithia springs also, with gushing streams of silver, good to drink and drink again.

The surrounding country is somewhat bleak, rough and mountainous. This might possibly bore some people who would miss bustle and crowds, but to anyone who loved nature, who could walk or ride on those mountain paths, nothing could give more perfect rest than this good hotel in its wild fastness, with these healing springs, and this mountain air, mild and comforting alike in winter weather or in summer shine.

"This bleakness and roughness of aspect, however, is nothing but the grim appearance, which we might attribute to some fabled dragon on guard at the portal of a concealed paradise. Before the venturesome the monster flees. We found such a paradise in an excursion we made to one of the many picturesque valleys in this mountain stretch. We drove in under the great trees until we were close to the dancing stream, which ran gayly on its course through the valley, leaping from rock to rock for our pleasure and diversion.

It was delightful to stray along the banks and to clamber out upon the rocks amid the turmoil of the torrent, and watch the cataract descend from crag to crag behind the veil of foliage which obscured and yet enhanced its beauty.

There is a feminine grace in all such beautiful scenes. The exquisite forms of the waving current, the crystal depths of the silent pools, the reflected lights within them of the heavens above, the fresh pure sparkle of the dancing waves, the snowy purity of the descending torrent, the freshness of the living foliage, the happy life of birds and flowers, all made glad by the presence of the stream, suggest the feminine idea, which ever gives life and grace and beauty to that which without it would be but a barren wilderness.

We got back from our excursion as evening fell down on the surrounding mountains, and after dinner passed some pleasant hours in the spacious parlors of the New Homestead Hotel. There, to our surprise and pleasure, we met some dear friends from New York.

This reminds me that during the day, as I was lounging about at the Springs, I saw approaching me a splendid-looking swell, gotten up in the highest style of riding costume—great baggy corduroys, with close-fitting leather leggings, a jaunty hat, a smart coat, and a riding whip in his hand. He was fair and florid, and well set up, with a flaunting yellow moustache of grand proportions, and had a general air of being excessively healthy and happy.

As this splendid vision came near me I ventured to give it a quiet and direct glance; when from the clear blue eyes came a look of recognition, and from the laughing mouth the words, "Well, if this isn't Canon Knowles!" My reply was: "M——, what on earth are you doing here?"

He soon told me that he was the riding-master at the hotel; that he had been at Hot Springs for quite a time. Here, said I to myself, is the right man in the right place at last. I had met him in New York, and admired his splendid appearance. He always seemed to me too manly and intelligent for the limited sphere in which he had found employment. It rejoiced me, then, to see him here, in his free, outdoor life and congenial occupation, which brought into full play the manly qualities so well developed on the genial soil of his native Ireland. I am sure that such a splendid fellow as this must be popular with his pupils, earnest and steady as he is, as well as gentle and polite.

In the early hours of the morning we descended the mountains and reached once more the main line, where we had to wait some hours for our train connection. Our stopping place was a wide plain, almost "Western" in its extent. There a city was to have been built. The name given thereto was suggestive of the foundations of all greatness. Speculation ran high; all was to be on a grand scale; and the little old village not far off cowered before the advent of the mighty city. But it never came. It was all shrunk up to nothing, or nearly so, and a weather-beaten street-car line, run by mule power, was the connecting link between the dead city and the living old hamlet away in the hills.

It would be sadly interesting if one could read the whole story of such a venture and its ultimate failure.

While we were waiting under the burning sun our car was an object of attraction to the boys playing about. Bright, clear-eyed little fellows they were, straight up and down, and independent. It was amusing to see the nonchalant way they interviewed us. They climbed upon the steps, they stood on the platform at the end, they entered and sat down; but all was done so undemonstratively and with such manly ease that we could not object.

We were interested in these little

Virginians—so manly, so simple, and so gentlemanly. There was nothing whatever boisterous or rude about them. They brought us wild flowers, and were not eager for remuneration. They waved us a farewell politely as our car sped away.

It took us many long hours to reach Luray, where late in the evening we entered the mystic regions underground, of which we will tell in the next chapter.

Luray Cavern

WITHIN the Holy Place of God
    The light of day did never shine ;
As if to tell that earthly light,
    He needed not within His shrine.

For light and dark to Him are one,
    He seeth where no light can be ;
And where no mortal eye can peer,
    He works with wondrous symmetry.

The crystal in the darkness dim,
    The gem within the depths of earth,
The treasures of the unseen world,
    Have each and all with Him their birth.

Thus, in this cavern huge and vast,
    And wondrous, with its splendors rare,
The darkness witnesses the truth,
    That God was ever working there.

J. H. K.

Saracen's Tent

VI

It was night when we reached the old-fashioned village of Luray, but that made the entrance into the famous caverns more romantic still.

Although the regular season had not opened we were most courteously met by the superintendent of the caves, an omnibus was placed at our disposal, and through the long, straggling village street we drove out a mile to the hillside entrance of the underground wonders.

Even in the dark it was a beautiful ride. The dimly lit village streets and the lights of homes seen through open windows were pleasant. The clear obscure of the open country under the stars had also its charms. Away eastward a huge conflagration was blazing on the distant mountains. In our eyes it seemed something terrible, but to our guide it was but a prosaic affair—only some folks burning out the underbrush to let the grass grow upon the mountains for the cattle thereon. Commonplace as its origin might have been it was a splendid illumination, nevertheless, and added to our enjoyment.

The guide was a charming fellow, with a refined good face. He was kindness itself to us, and took all pains possible in showing us the wonders of the caverns. His gentlemanliness was manifest in every turn. The flames in the far distance suggested to my mind the long past warlike scenes of the Shenandoah Valley in which we then were. I asked our guide if he had recollections of those bitter days. "Yes," said he, "I remember them well. It was nothing but trouble for years. We scarcely knew how to get bread for our families, or how to keep it if we had it. We were run over by both armies, time and time again, until we were sick of our lives." There was an infinite pathos in his introspective look, as he brought up the memories of the past which the blazing hillside had suggested to my mind.

We reached the entrance to the caves, a well-appointed house built over a descending staircase which led directly to the wonders. Here American refinement and ingenuity met us on the threshold. We were given candles, but these were not merely single ones, which each could take in his or her hand. No, they were arranged in clusters of three or four, placed in a combined socket. Attached to this socket was a curved metal shade, to which was fastened a convenient handle. The upright shade covered the light from one's eyes, the handle made it pleasant to hold, all dripping of grease was prevented, and with complete comfort we could follow our guide down the steps into the cavern.

We were told that there was no mud, no dirt, no danger; all that was necessary and peremptory was that we were to keep close to our guide, and by no means to step aside into any alluring by-paths. Good advice this, for any undertaking, to keep to the prescribed way and to keep close also to one's leader.

The caverns during the show season are lit with electric lamps, but the illumination which our guide provided seemed to me better than any steady electric light could be. We saw the caves by means of a plentiful use of magnesium wire.

As we advanced through the first cavern our candles revealed to us somewhat of the Aladdin-like wonders of the fairy place, but when our guide flashed out his bright white light, and waved it about over the glittering stalactites and the grotesque and wonderful formations on every hand, the effect was magical. To this bright light would succeed the darkness of the abyss, until our eyes could again perceive the flare of our candles, which served to illuminate but a narrow circle and show us one step at a time.

We were taken from one wonder to another, up and down again, until we had reached a depth of over two hundred feet. There was no damp, nothing disagreeable, the air was pure and sweet, and not too cold. We saw glittering formations in all kinds of fantastic shapes, some clear and white as the purest moonlight, others rose-colored, others gray, others tinted like onyx, and grained like the finest wood, varying in tone from richest brown to brightest orange.

We saw clear pools of pellucid water, silent, cold, and still, like fairies' mirrors. Some were like huge cups partly crusted over by a carbonate film, others were fifty feet deep or more.

All sorts of fantastic names were given to the formations, such as Titania's Bower, Saladin's Tent, and the Spectre, or anything which the fancy might contrive; but the silence of it all, and the carving work done in the eternal darkness, were more to me than mere names.

Here one could see, descending

from the unseen heights, huge laminæ, side by side, close and regular as the underside of a mushroom, but huge as giant oaks; yet, monstrous as they were, as delicately moulded as a lady's ear.

Here was a prostrate giant, a huge column of alabaster, gnawed and discolored by the ages which had recorded the unknown years since its overthrow. In and around and through it all we wandered in the surrounding darkness, led on by our faithful guide. Our candles, shining out before our own footsteps, but yet keeping ourselves ever in the shade, produced many curious groupings. These were all enhanced when, at point after point, the magnesium wire flashed out its weird white light for our surprise and delight.

It was a sensation to look into the mazy black depths utterly beyond our reach. In one of these we could dimly discern the embedded bones of a human skeleton, some hapless one who in forgotten ages dropped down there to his irrevocable doom.

What a fate it must have been to be thus buried alive in impenetrable darkness, within those cold smooth walls which no mortal foot could ever climb.

Had he wandered in from the outward world, and lost his way, or had he dropped from above down through some half-concealed fissure which opened to the upper air?

It might have been in some such fashion as this latter, for it was by observing such a fissure, through which cold air seemed to rush upward, that the caverns were discovered by Mr. Andrew J. Campbell, who, with others, entered them on August 13, 1878. Since then the caverns have been a showplace of great attraction, thousands visiting them every year. They are certainly worth more than one visit; for in beauty and richness the stalactite display exceeds that of any other cavern known.

The immense space called the ball-room suggests the magnificence of a race of giants. The rocks above, with their clustering pendants catching the light; the great decorations of encrusted alabaster upon cyclopean walls; the great oval of the cemented floor, the seats arranged here and there for spectators; give the notion that if one were to wait in silence and utter some magic spell the mysterious denizens of this strange palace would show themselves to our mortal gaze, and make rare revel for our delight and awe.

Neither would music be wanting. Every hanging frond of crystal is an instrument ready to answer with a touch. The great stalactites would give a tone deep as the lowest organ note, and the whole gamut of musical utterance could be evoked by a knowing hand.

We heard this litho-melody to perfection in the vast opening called the cathedral. Our guide left us grouped at one side of the great space, while on the other he approached the organ, formed of alabaster columns closely placed together. He played a little melody which was weird in the stillness, and as he plied his hammer rapidly over the whole surface, as one would slide the finger over piano keys, he showed us that a patient and skilful musician could find every tone and semitone necessary for any melody or complicated harmony. Our guide was more successful with the cathedral chimes, which he struck out from some huge sword-like pendants near by. The tone was clear and true, producing in that semi-darkness an effect which one could never forget.

We were told that the extent of these caverns in all their wonder is unknown. Every year new chambers are opened and made ready for inspection. A certain amount of clearing has to be done, but I begged of our guide that portions at least should be left entirely in the rough. Thereupon he conducted us into a part not yet thrown open to the public. It was like the forest primeval. The dust of ages was there, the uncleared floor littered with débris, the ooze under foot, the precarious treading which needed constant watchfulness, but the glory of stalactite and crystal was all the same. I was satisfied when I saw this cavern absolutely untouched, that the improvements of cement paths to walk on, of fence-posts and railing, and other marks of human care, did not take anything from the unequalled beauties of the Luray Cavern.

"Geologically considered, the

Luray Cavern does not date beyond the tertiary period, though carved from the Silurian limestone. At some period long subsequent to its original excavation, and after many large stalactites had grown, it was completely filled with glacial mud charged with acid, whereby the dripstone was eroded into singularly grotesque shapes. After the mud had been mostly removed by flowing water, these eroded forms remained among the new growths. To this contrast may be ascribed some of the most striking scenes in the cave. The many and extraordinary monuments of aqueous energy include massive columns wrenched from their place in the ceiling and prostrate on the floor; the hollow column, forty feet high and thirty feet in diameter, standing erect, but pierced by a tubular passage from top to bottom; the leaning column, nearly as large, undermined and tilting like the campanile of Pisa; the organ, a cluster of stalactites dropped points downward in the room known as the cathedral; besides a vast bed of disintegrated carbonates left by the whirling flood in the retreat known as the Elfin Ramble." *

It would be impossible to over-

* Encyclopædia Britannica, art. "Luray Cavern."

estimate the richness and grandeur of those underground wonders in Luray Cavern. In the canopy alone of the Imperial Spring it is estimated that 40,000 pendants are visible at once.

For hours one may traverse this land of gnomes and pixies, and yet leave the scene, as we did, with the feeling that the half had not been told us, and that we had seen but the merest fragment of its unending wonders.

Harper's Ferry

It seems a place filled with pure upper air,
   An open gateway to the golden west,
   A garden fair, hemmed in by mountain crest,
With some kind faithful dragon watching there.

O ever may, the products fair, of peace,
   The golden apples meet for marriage feast,
   Of union true, 'twixt West, North, South and
      East,
Grow in our Hesper-land, and never cease.

And may they also ever guarded be
   By faithful hearts, the loyal and the true ;
   And may these golden apples aye renew
Our love of country and of liberty.

                                 J. H. K.

Harper's Ferry

VII

As we were drawing near Harper's Ferry a brakeman entered our car and drew our attention to Charlestown, Virginia, which we were then approaching.

"That dome," said the brakeman, "is where John Brown was tried, and not far off he was hung." The quiet old town, which seemed to show no signs of modern progress, at once assumed an interest in our eyes. For think what one may of John Brown and his actions at Harper's Ferry, October, 1859, he stands out as the advancing herald of events which began to take place in all their dread reality eighteen months after his death.

A man who could stand on the gallows in that town of Charlestown, with the black cap drawn over his face and the noosed rope about his neck for a long fifteen minutes, while troops were marched and countermarched to form a hollow square about his gibbet, without ever showing a quiver, either in head or in arm or limb, must have had some stuff in him. Yet that was the process of his taking off, when, after the sheriff left him with the word that all was ready, he was thus left in that awful darkness awaiting the coming of his doom.

The man was the product of his inheritance and environments. He was saturated with the Bible; he brooded on the ideas of liberty; he was a mystic himself; he deemed himself an instrument in the hands of God for the work that he set out to do. Had he broken with orthodoxy and put himself forward as a leader in a new religion, his force and gloomy power might have had results as enormous as that of Joseph Smith and Brigham Young, both, alike with John Brown, products strangely sprung from certain conditions of American life.

I remember well the thrill which passed through the country in 1859 when the leader of the Harper's Ferry raid and his comrades were hung by the State of Virginia. Some applauded the short and sharp decision which seemed happily to end the whole disturbing matter. Others felt otherwise, and sadly said, "The end is not yet." No one knew what was coming.

It is worth while quoting here

what Governor Wise, of Virginia, wrote concerning John Brown: "They are mistaken who take John Brown to be a madman. He is a bundle of the best nerves I ever saw; cut and thrust and bleeding and in bonds. He is a man of clear head, of courage, fortitude and simple ingenuousness. He is cool, collected, indomitable; and it is but just to him to say that he was humane to his prisoners, and he inspired me with great trust in his integrity as a man of truth." This opinion, coming from a gentleman in high position, whose duty it was to have him tried, duly sentenced and hung, is of some weight.

With all these ghosts of the past in our minds, we reached picturesque Harper's Ferry, and as we crowded out on our car platform to look about us, one of our party exclaimed, with feeling voice, "This is Harper's Ferry, where that great and good man John Brown made his noble stand for freedom."

Near us was a small group of men, one of whom looked up in a quick, nervous manner, and replied at once with a tone like the ping of a rifle: "Sir, I feel sorry for you if you can call Brown a good man; he was the ——— rascal God Almighty ever put breath into. He came here and tried to steal our property; and, right over there, within thirty rods of us, he shot down innocent men in cold blood."

This sudden aspect of a totally different view of things was absolutely ludicrous. The seriousness of the fact that such views do exist was as nothing. The words were hailed with a roar of laughter from all sides. Then, after a blank silence of surprise, there was some more talk *pro* and *con*. It was soon all over.

I confess that I felt some sympathy with my well-knit, firmly set old mountaineer from Virginia, as he hurled back in his calm rage his last shot: "Why didn't you buy our slaves from us and not rob us of everything we had?" There the hardy old fellow stood, defiant looking and yet gentlemanly. He had in his hands a superb bouquet of mountain azalea, which seemed to emphasize the finer side of his nature, even while his clear eye flashed lightning. To ease matters a little I stepped off the car and engaged him in conversation about the charming flowers he was holding. With hospitable grace he handed me the whole bunch. I thanked him and said that they would serve as a peace offering in the present dispute. Quite close to the station was a small obelisk set up to mark the site of John Brown's fortress, and hard by, where the American flag was flying in the breeze, was the place where the blood had been shed to which the Virginian had referred.

Curiously enough, a few days before leaving New York I met a gentleman who mentioned to me, I do not remember in what connection, that John Brown in his younger days was a believer in non-resistance, and the literal interpretation of the ethics of the Sermon on the Mount, but after his Kansas experience he deliberately made the Old Testament his model—an eye for an eye, and a tooth for a tooth. This accounts for the assassination in Kansas of the four pro-slavery men called from their beds at night and deliberately shot. It also explains the strangeness of his actions at Harper's Ferry, which, as we now look back at them, merely antedated a huge movement later on, which drenched the entire nation with blood.

Our brief stay at Harper's Ferry, short as it was, seemed a continuation of the history of the nation. We soon drew out from the station and left the romantic spot far behind.

The rest of our day's journey was through the lovely valley of the Shenandoah, peaceful in its

Valley of the Shenandoah

fertile slopes, encompassed by the distant hills, and watered by the winding river.

All was once the scene of weary warfare, now for ever ended. How hard it was to realize, amid the present beauty and rest, the fire and smoke of contending forces and the horror and tears of suffering and of death.

Washington

Like some huge tower of soaring silver flame,
    The Obelisk lifts high its awful form,
    Radiant, serene, in sunshine or in storm,
It tells of him, who gives to it, his name.

Silent, serene, unmoved and ever true,
    Like silver tried in sevenfold furnace fires,
    His spirit still our faltering will inspires,
And summons us, like him, to dare and do.

The curving dome, may speak of pliant wills;
    The colonnades, of whispering intrigues;
    But, brave, the Obelisk, doth such base leagues,
Frown down upon, with all their kindred ills.

Upward, severe, unswerving, honest, pure,
    A solemn sermon set in soaring stone;
    From time, it calls to God's eternal throne,
Where only what is pure, shall sure, endure.

                              J. H. K.

The Ménage

VIII

It was well on in the afternoon when we reached Washington, and, having the next day before us, a good rest was the wisest proceeding. This I obtained while riding at random on some of the street-car lines, where one can look about and see people and things without much fatigue.

At night I happened upon a capital specimen of negro music. I was strolling on one of the streets near the station, just before turning in for the night in our railroad car, when I heard some sweet sounds coming from a dark corner near a vacant lot. In the gloom I could see three negro youngsters lying on the grass, crooning their melodies for their own delight. A little crowd soon gathered, and the singers were induced, by the hope of some dimes, to step into the light and raise their music in louder fashion. This they did with a will, varying their performance with wild dances. There was a survival of the barbaric in the tom-tom slapping on the thigh to mark time for the dancers; while in the music there was a strange tone, full of mystery.

The three boys, when singing, formed a group, facing inward. They stared into each other's eyes as if possessed, and then they warbled away in a three-part harmony, always pleasing, sometimes a little crude, but again and again introducing curious diminutions and expansions of interval, more like the gypsy music of Hungary or Bohemia than aught else. A few of the melodies I heard were genuine darky airs; others were ordinary music-hall songs, but given with a peculiar twist by these young minstrels.

During the winter I had heard a delightful concert by the Mendelssohn Glee Club, of New York, in which some negro music was admirably sung. Beautiful as it was it lacked the wild flavor of the genuine article, such as one could perceive in the untutored efforts of these street lads. If the three boys in Washington could be induced to sing on the New York concert stage just as they sang in the shadow of a fence, as I heard them, it would make a success.

As the little *al fresco* concert was at full blast a cry came on the night air, "Cheese it, the cop!" and the three darky performers fluttered off into the outer darkness like frightened birds.

A day at Washington, and at

such a place, how little it is to have at one's disposal! But a wise traveller will never lament over what he cannot see, and will limit his observations to his opportunity and be philosophically content therewith.

The Congressional Library was our first point, we had heard so much of its splendor and its greatness. It is indeed a magnificent affair. The exterior has a quiet sumptuousness most satisfactory, and the interior fairly glows with rich color and decoration. There is so much of this that it is almost oppressive. The loud tone of the entrance hall, the gay coloring, and the flaunting forwardness of that part seem to call for a shout of exultation rather than for the reverent hush which one might be expected to experience when approaching the sacred shrine of Minerva. The inner corridors are, some of them, exquisite models in subdued and appropriate coloring, and the whole place, outside of the library proper, is a library in itself, full of thought and art, an ever open book for all comers. One could tread those courts for years and find new lessons in each reprise of footstep.

From the surrounding gallery of the great rotunda we looked down into the library far below. Up near where we stood were great monumental bronze figures of famous men of the past. Beneath was the broad silent space, filled in with the busy workers of the present, as in their sumptuous surroundings they toiled amid their books.

The whole effect of the library was rich in the extreme. The superb rotunda, with its vast lantern, the bronzes, the marbles, the carvings, the decorations, the sumptuous quiet of the place, suggested an infinity of wealth and power. There was a pomp and circumstance about it all as if of something triumphant. It made me think of Venice in its glory, and of the grandeur of the Roman basilicas, of the luxuriousness of old Italian ceilings and ornamentation. It was with a corrective shock that one thought of the Radcliffe Library at Oxford, or the old Bodleian, or of the simple uncompromising plainness of the huge rotunda of the British Museum. I doubt if the austerity of the old British Museum would ever please our people. We seem to need the magnificent and the splendid; a note of luxury and pomp is ever with us in our private life as well as in our public affairs. In Washington itself there is, however, a simple and unaffected side which is truly wonderful.

Nowhere do you see any evidence of display, military or official. Here are no horseguards mounted as immovable sentries before buildings of state; no soldiers passing their rounds before the residence of President or members of the cabinet; not a vestige of anything of the kind. You pass by the White House, the Treasury, the Capitol, or any other public building: not a guard is in evidence anywhere. Of course there are caretakers and detectives and all that, for such are necessary against accident. The whole air of Washington seems to say: "Everything here is in the guardianship of the people."

We had several drives through

the ever varying avenues and squares of this beautiful Washington. The wealth of foliage, the broad spaces, and the splendor of the public and private buildings, with their picturesque groupings, impress one with the attractiveness of this queen city of the nation.

The growing heat reminded us that we must not be lured on to undue exertion, and we concluded to limit our excursions to a visit to the great obelisk.

A closer view of this great structure, which dominates the landscape with a sort of spiritual splendor for miles about Washington, impressed us greatly.

It is a fearful sensation to stand close to its vast height and then look up to its huge walls. The optical effect is bewildering and almost uncanny. We had hoped to make the ascent, but the elevator was out of order, and it was too near the hour of closing to make an attempt to get at the top by the staircase.

The exclamation of a gentleman who had just returned from a pilgrimage to the summit, and his earnest manner in saying "I would not do that again for a farm," spread contentment among us at our failure to make the ascent.

A curious effect was to experience the rush of cold air blown out through the entrance door from the heights above. It came like a breeze from the northland, and with an intensity quite remarkable.

While looking at the great obelisk close to its base, one feels that the smallness of the blocks has, near the ground, a rather weak effect, and yet I suppose it could not have been otherwise. Perhaps the uniformity of the stones suggests universal suffrage and the equality of all votes. Some courses of larger blocks in the first stages of the building would have been more satisfying to the eye. The chipping away and disintegration of those small courses of the marble, so easily noticeable, gives one an uncomfortable suggestion.

The plain square doorway, too, seems a mean sort of thing. I would like to see the base, for at least twenty or thirty feet up, enclosed in handsome bronze, forming a great ornamental frieze of State flags and emblems, or, better yet, a spirited grouping of all the heroes of the Revolution, with Washington himself in their midst. Such a frieze of noble men would be an eternal object lesson in history, and take away from the mean effect of the lower portion of the great obelisk, and also remove the cold isolation of having

Washington all by himself and not rather with his generals around him, without whom even he could not have been what he was.

Our day in Washington was soon to end, and then, some time in the night, our train was to whisk us away to New York while we slept.

It so happened that a great event coincided with our stay of a day. We read it in the evening papers. It was the payment to Spain of twenty million dollars in connection with the formal cession of the Philippine Islands to the United States. The papers told us of the four checks for $5,-000,000 each, and how the French

Ambassador, M. Cambon, received them at the State Department, giving a receipt therefor, nonchalantly folding up the four precious pieces of paper in his card case, putting that in his pocket and returning to his home quite unattended and on foot, without the slightest concern about the vast sum he carried with him. The receipt which M. Cambon gave was dated May 1, 1899, and was as follows:

"Received from the Secretary of State of the United States the sum of twenty million dollars ($20,000,000) in four drafts upon the treasurer of the United States, numbered 4,509, 4,510, 4,511, 4,512, and dated April 29, 1899, each draft being for five million dollars ($5,000,000), the same being in full payment of the obligation of the Government of the United States to the Government of Spain, as set forth in Article III. of the treaty of peace between the United States and Spain, signed at Paris, France, on the 10th day of December, eighteen hundred and ninety-eight, the ratifications of which were exchanged in the city of Washington, on the 11th day of April, one thousand eight hundred and ninety-nine, the same being provided by an act of Congress, approved March 2, 1899, entitled 'An act making appropriations to carry out the obligations of the treaty between the United States and Spain, concluded December 10, eighteen hundred and ninety-eight.'"

What an illustration the whole proceeding was of the quietness and confidence of these

United States. The utter simplicity of the whole proceeding—the French Ambassador walking to the State Department and returning to his embassy again on foot, the huge affair and all its relations, transpiring as a mere commonplace transaction—it was splendid.

A little over a year ago our party passed through Washington for our "Flight in Spring." The war with Spain was not then declared, but war was in the air. Now the whole great action was over, the war was ended; the payment to M. Cambon, who represented Spain, finished the whole transaction.

We were out on the Pacific coast during April and May of last year. While the war was at its height we followed its progress with throbbing hearts, hearing by the shores of the Pacific of the glorious victories of our fleet on the far opposite shores. We felt, out there in California, as never before, the glory and splendor of our great land. It all grew upon us as we traversed its empire from east to west, and back again to east, to New York, and to home.

Again we had been on our travels. We were speeding from Summer Land to Summer, passing through a portion of the vast

States of the South, back again to New York and to home, and our new journey was to us a fresh revelation of the unimagined wonders of this our land wherever one is happy enough to pass over, in any direction, its vast extent, rich and glorious as it is, and freighted with possibilities for the future, possibilities which they alone who even in some dim way know America can ever faintly imagine.

Our night between Washington and Jersey City passed like a dream. In the early morning hours we were ferried across to Liberty Street, and once more New York received us into the immensity of its undimmed magnificence. Our trip from Summer Land to Summer was at an end.

www.ingramcontent.com/pod-product-compliance
Lightning Source LLC
Chambersburg PA
CBHW031828230426
43669CB00009B/1269